The Plague
of the Black Debt

by James Dale Davidson

How to Survive the Coming Depression

You've read about them in *The Wall Street Journal, The Economist, Financial Times, Barron's, The Washington Post,* and *USA Today*...

James Dale Davidson

Davidson is a principal in Strategic Advisors Corporation, an asset management group for wealthy individuals. His worldwide contacts with bankers, multinational fund managers, and important public officials enable him to make bold forecasts — based on information from those who are in a position to see and profit from major financial trends.

Davidson's most recent book (co-authored with Lord Rees-Mogg) is *The Great Reckoning*, a look at the end of the post-war world and the coming bankruptcy of the welfare state.

In 1987, he and Lord Rees-Mogg co-wrote *Blood in the Streets*, which accurately forecast the crash that occurred only months later.

Currently chairman of the National Taxpayers Union and director of the Pembroke College Foundation, he has appeared on *The Tonight Show* as well as many other leading TV programs. He is an Advisor on Economic Reform to one of the former Soviet Republics. He holds degrees in economics and political science from the University of Maryland and Oxford University.

Lord William Rees-Mogg

Former editor-in-chief of *The Times of London*, Rees-Mogg has an uncanny ability to predict investment opportunities.

Rees-Mogg teamed up with Davidson in 1984 to produce *Strategic Investment* newsletter. Their ability to analyze seemingly chaotic markets and to discover profitable opportunities made the newsletter an overnight success.

At home in England, Rees-Mogg is prominently positioned in the British public eye. He is a member of the House of Lords, vice chairman of the BBC and chairman of the Broadcast Standards Council, which sets standards for public broadcasting.

He was chairman of the British delegation on implementing the Helsinki Accords and was Chairman of the Arts Council of Great Britain. He is advisor to some of the wealthiest families in Europe, and a confidant of Margaret Thatcher.

His forecasts are based on his thorough understanding of geopolitical forces combined with his personal contacts with the high-powered decision makers in the world of international finance. In fact, Rees-Mogg's extensive information network has been termed an "investor's CIA."

CONTENTS _____

Chapter One

Three Little Charts
And the Coming
"End of the World"

You don't have to be a conservative, a liberal, or anything at all to understand that America is about to be flattened by a tidal wave. Just consider the following chart:

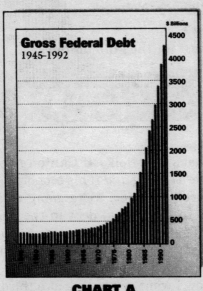

CHART A

Pretty bad, huh? Now consider a second chart:

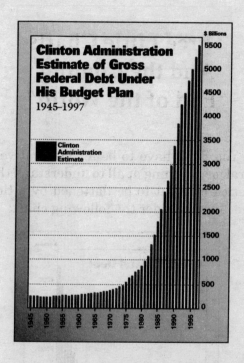

That's right, folks. If Clinton gets everything he's asking *and* if his economic projections are on target, we're going to add $1 trillion to the federal debt in the next four years. That's more than George Bush added in his four years. And it's almost as much as Reagan added in *eight* years.

Now I want you to look at a third chart.

These are *my* projections:

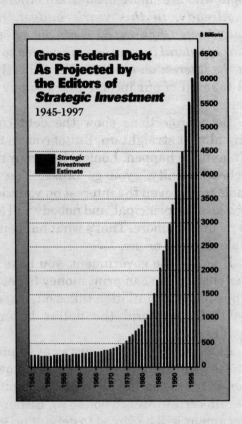

Gross Federal Debt As Projected by the Editors of *Strategic Investment*

1945–1997

Strategic Investment Estimate

$ Billions

There you have it. It's a graphic picture of a freight train — and it's headed towards *you*.

It doesn't matter whether you prefer my figures or Bill Clinton's. We're merely talking about different shades of disaster. When you're dead you're dead. There aren't some people who are "more dead" than others.

Already, in this year's budget, with Clinton's own figures, 57 cents out of every dollar of federal income taxes is needed to pay just the interest on the debt. Very shortly, it will take all of our income taxes to pay the interest.

Both projections show the debt curve going almost straight up. But of course that isn't going to happen. Long before your debt reaches "infinity," you go broke. You are unable to pay even the interest on your debt, much less the principal, and nobody will lend you money anymore. That's what happens to people like you or me.

If you're the government, you have another choice: You can print money to get out of your fix. Then inflation takes off, interest rates take off, and the dollar becomes worthless.

At most, we're a few years away from one of these grim scenarios. It is *too late* now to reverse the situation. President Clinton's program certainly does not do so. Either the government will be forced to default on such obligations as Social Security, Medicare, and military pensions. Or the government will pay everything in full — with worthless money. In a moment, I'll tell you more about which one it's going to be.

Short term here are some events I expect in the next few months:

➤ The public will learn that unemployment is actually growing 50% *faster* than last year. The numbers we're getting now are false.

➤ Boris Yeltsin will lose his job. Russia will come under the control of a nationalist, militarist regime — in effect, a fascist regime. Disruptions in the former Soviet Union will upset Western markets.

➤ The price of oil will fall below $15 per barrel.

➤ U.S. stocks in '93: Down. Bonds: Down. Interest rates: Up.

➤ First-time investors have poured money into the market over the last two years. They'll pull it out at the first sign of trouble, creating a downward spiral.

➤ The Japanese crisis will deepen. Unemployment there will reach record levels. They will have a major banking crisis. The Japanese will try to raise cash by dumping their American "trophy properties," like Rockefeller Center.

➤ Saddam Hussein has replaced almost
  all the arms he lost in the Gulf War.
  He will test Clinton's resolve in a
  major way — soon.

It's urgent that you take action *now*. The
purpose of this book is to help you decide
what to do to protect yourself — and to even
get rich during the coming bad years!

❧

Chapter Two _____

1930 All Over Again

History repeats itself, often in startling ways. But, you can know in advance. . . you can understand. . . and you can profit from these predictable patterns. This book will show you how.

The world is shaped by big, powerful forces or trends that nobody can control and that 999 out of 1,000 people don't even see. However, if you know what the trends are, you *can* reap tremendous wealth. Usually (but not always) these forces are driven by technology.

And I'll jump ahead just a little bit and tell you something else: The forces at work right now are driving the biggest change in 500 years. Terrible suffering is going to occur. But big money is going to be made at the same time.

People didn't know in 1800 that they were living in the Industrial Revolution. Someone came along fifty years later, gave it a name, and explained what had happened. In 1930, they didn't know they were in the Great

Depression. They thought the problems would soon blow over. They didn't
know there is a 60-year debt cycle.
Since the mid-16th century there have
been nine depressions.

There were depressions in the 1820s, the
1870s, and the 1930s. Europe is in a depression now. Japan is in deep trouble.

They say a picture is worth a thousand
words. So I'm going to save about 975 words
and show you the best picture I can find of the
60-year cycle.

The chart on the facing page shows you
the ups and downs in the most important
measure of the money supply, going all the
way back to 1900. It bothers me a great deal.
It ought to bother you, too.

It shows that growth in the money supply has put in a massive top just like the
1930s.

What's the big deal about money supply?
It's the most important predictor of stock
market performance, inflation, and growth
in the economy. Every economist and savvy
investor watches the money supply like a
hawk. The power of the monetary indicators
swamps every other numerical indicator.

Martin Zweig, one of the smartest investors on Wall Street, says, "Don't fight the
Fed. . .In the stock market, as with horse

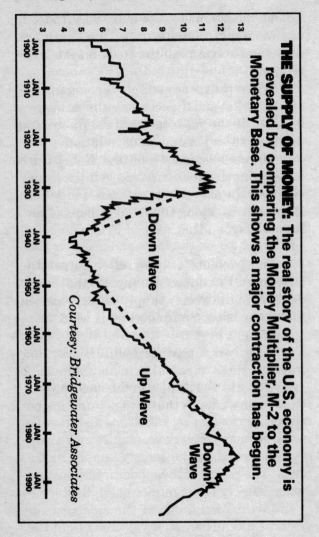

THE SUPPLY OF MONEY: The real story of the U.S. economy is revealed by comparing the Money Multiplier, M-2 to the Monetary Base. This shows a major contraction has begun.

Courtesy: Bridgewater Associates

racing, money makes the mare go. . .Indeed, the monetary climate. . . is the dominant factor in determining the stock market's direction."

When the money supply is going up, the stock market and the economy almost always do well. If the monetary indicators are *too* positive, there's a danger of inflation.

Milton Friedman won the Nobel prize for showing that *too much growth* in the money supply is the *only* thing that causes inflation. It took them a long time, but policy makers finally learned that part of Friedman's lesson.

The problem is, they often forget the other part. Friedman also showed that sharp *declines* in the money supply cause recession and depression. Sharp decline is what we're seeing right now.

History is repeating itself. Usually, low interest rates mean the money supply is growing. But as I'll show in the next chapter, that wasn't true in the 1930s — and it's not true now.

❧

Chapter Three _____

Low Interest Rates
Are Luring Investors
Over a Cliff

The chart in the last chapter shows money supply falling like a rock, just as it did at the beginning of the Great Depression. While most "experts" are looking for inflation to make a comeback, the most important indicator is signaling deflation!

"No problem," you might say. The Federal Reserve controls the money supply, and the Fed is pursuing a "loose" monetary policy.

Well, the answer to that is this: The Fed has been pursuing a loose money policy for three years, and the money supply is *still* falling like a rock. The Fed has moved heaven and earth to get the money supply up, and it's not working.

It has reduced interest rates 24 times in the last three years. It has pumped reserves into the banking system. It is "creating" money out of thin air at the rate of a billion dollars a week by buying Treasury bills.

And it's not working.

There's something else: The Fed did the

same thing in the '30s. And it didn't work then, either. Right now, the markets are confused because interest rates are going down, and that is always good for the stock market. At least that's what people think.

There has only been one other time when interest rates and money supply plunged at the same time: The early 1930s, the first years of the Great Depression.

After the Crash of 1929, the Fed immediately dropped interest rates from six percent to five percent. Within two weeks, the rate had been pushed down to 4.5 percent. By March 1930, it stood at 3.5 percent. By 1933, Treasury securities yielded one-half of one percent! Yet the overall money supply collapsed and continued to fall for years.

A great many investors are banking on low interest rates to keep the economy growing and the stock market pumped up. They are going to receive the shock of the century.

History *does* repeat itself. It *is* repeating itself.

Do not assume "everything is going to be all right." It's not. Let's take a stroll through America as it will be just a few years from now.

๛

Chapter Four

The Plague of the Black Debt
(Plus the Most Profitable Investment in the U.S.)

In three years, from 1347-50, about one person out of every three in Europe died of bubonic plague. This was the famous Black Death. Whole villages were wiped out, left to return to the wilderness. In cities, thousands of houses were boarded up and deserted.

I call the coming disaster in America the Plague of the Black *Debt*. No, I don't expect millions to die (although it's possible if society collapses).

What I do expect is that the world will be changed, totally and permanently. Things will never be the same again.

➤ I see Social Security benefits being cut to the bone. They'll probably only go to the most needy.

➤ I see at least 40 million unemployed or in make-work public assistance jobs.

➤ Sick elderly will be cared for at home.
Almost no one will be able to afford
nursing home care.

➤ I see millions of homeowners "upside
down" — with the mortgage bigger
than the market value of the home. A
lot of them will hand the key to the
lender and walk away. There will be a
lot of empty houses with "For Sale"
signs.

➤ Banking industry problems will return, much worse than anything we've
seen. And much too big next time for
the government to bail out. Either
your savings will be wiped out or you'll
be paid in worthless paper dollars.

➤ I expect to see "extended families" of
10 to 15 crammed into three-bedroom
houses. Millions of retired folks will
be forced to live with their children.
Young people in their twenties and
thirties — including young marrieds
with their children — will move in
with their parents. In many cases, not
a person in the house will have a full-
time job.

Picture yourself in a suburban neighborhood where the houses on either side of you
are empty and for sale. Windows are broken

out. Homeless and squatters break in and sleep there. There are no police to stop them because local government is broke and the tax base has fallen sharply.

For the same reason, the streets are full of potholes and streetlights are broken. Power outages are common. In this dark, menacing environment, crime runs wild.

Almost everyone drives a "clunker" because few people can afford a new car anymore. Mountains of green garbage bags pile up, stinking to heaven, because it's three weeks between trash pick-ups. In short. . . the suburbs will become slums. It has already happened in communities that went broke. It is going to happen in a great many more communities.

Somebody Will Still Be Rich. Will It Be You?

It doesn't give me any pleasure to predict these things. But I want to get this information out to as many people as I can. . . because you *can* prepare yourself. You and those you love can avoid this catastrophe. And the more of us who preserve our wealth, the better it will be for our country when the time comes to rebuild.

Fortunately, you won't be one of the people stuck in the decaying neighborhood I described — if you heed my warnings and read my newsletter, STRATEGIC INVEST-MENT (see page 115 to order). Picture this:

> Two hours or so away from major cities, you are living in a sparkling clean resort community. Your assets are intact, and in fact they are worth more than ever. You don't need to live in a big town. Computer, fax, modem, telephone, and two-way interactive video connect you with like-minded people all over the world. You not only work but even shop, take courses, and visit your doctor through the com-munications network.

Along with other people who have high-level skills, you make a killing in the knowledge industries of the 21st century. Your most valuable asset is between your ears.

No, you aren't necessarily an engineer or a software genius. You may be an advertising executive, a writer, an artist, a venture capitalist, a money manager, a mail-order entrepreneur, a TV producer, a physical trainer, or a healthcare professional (in-cluding a host of new "alternative" therapies). Maybe your only job will be investing the money you're going to make in the next few years with the advance information you learn in STRATEGIC INVESTMENT.

Whatever you do, you've checked out of the collapsing welfare state.

This is your wake-up call. Pack your bags and check out *now*.

Is this too alarming? Some of our critics would say so. But last year during the Presidential primaries I ran into one of the Democratic contenders, a very well-known politician. He was jogging on the streets of my neighborhood, a wealthy Washington suburb, a few blocks from his posh hotel.

His question to me: "You still live here? Are you nuts? This city is going to burn." He couldn't believe I lived near "ground zero" of the coming social disorders. (As it happens, I was just renting. And I've moved since then.)

You see, the Establishment knows what's going on. Or at least some of its members do.

The Most Profitable Investment in the United States

There's a profit angle here, too, besides protecting your keester from the coming urban unrest. Small communities two hours away from major cities are the fastest-appreciating real estate in the country.

These communities are already benefiting from the "Fifth Migration" in American history. The "Third Migration" was from the farms to the cities, and the fourth (1950-70) was from cities to suburbs. Now, people like us are bailing out and moving to small, clean, safe towns. Technology makes it possible for us to work anywhere.

This is already a "happening thing" as the young folks say. You can find shops that rival Rodeo Drive. . .and elegant French restaurants. . .in dozens of communities no gang member has ever heard of.

Even if you're not ready to move yet, a rental property in these areas is the best investment in the United States. If you like to ski, you're really in luck. Environmentalists are preventing new ski resorts from being built, and real estate in existing resorts is soaring. (When you subscribe to STRATEGIC INVESTMENT, I'll send you a list of counties poised to profit from the Fifth Migration. See page 115.)

How do I know all this? What's the proof?

I'm glad you asked. Please turn to the next chapter.

≈

Chapter Five _____

Where We Get
Our Information:
An Investor's CIA

Almost twenty years ago, I founded a group called the National Taxpayers Union. We've been sounding the alarm about deficits ever since. NTU has grown to become one of the most powerful citizens organizations in the United States.

Our 250,000 members are citizens who are sick of taxes and deficits. We've fought every single tax increase.

My involvement with this group has given me access to America's most powerful people. The fact that I went to Oxford — as Bill Clinton did — has also given me valuable contacts. Right now, though, I'm not writing you as a representative of NTU but as a private person who's worried that we're facing another great depression.

I've written several books on America's economic and social crisis. Along with my war against taxes and deficits, my forecasts have earned me frequent invitations on programs like Good Morning America, the Tonight Show, and MacNeil-Lehrer.

In 1984 I founded a newsletter called *Strategic Investment* with Lord William Rees-Mogg. Rees-Mogg is the former editor-in-chief of *The Times of London,* Vice Chairman of the BBC, and confidant of powerful British figures like Margaret Thatcher and Lord Rothschild. He is also a director of London's Private Bank and financial advisor to some of the world's wealthiest families.

But most of all, we like to read books. We study history. True, we're economists and investment advisors, and we have very useful connections in politics, finance, and the intelligence community. But our hobby, what we love best, is studying the past and using it to forecast the future. We'd do this even if it didn't pay a cent.

History *does* repeat itself, as I said earlier. In this book, I want to show you exactly *how* it repeats itself and what now lies ahead. You can reap the benefit of our years of research.

Sometimes the cycles are quite precise and mathematical. Other times we have to read hundreds of books and apply seasoned judgment to see where the trends are headed.

We use these two approaches, plus a third method: the information we gather from our worldwide network of powerful, well-informed contacts.

An Investor's CIA

A deep knowledge of history is important. Computerized economic modeling is important. But it's our powerful network of people all over the world that gives us (and our readers) the edge.

As I'm sure you know, tips from "friends in high places" can make you huge amounts of money. For example. . .

Shortly after we founded STRATEGIC INVESTMENT in 1984, we became convinced that communism was about to fall apart. We decided to find out more. Tapping into our connections, we learned that a phone call had been placed from Finland to London.

The call was from a man employed as a chauffeur in the Russian Embassy in Helsinki (later identified as a KGB general). He was asking for help on behalf of a little-known member of the Soviet Politburo named Mikhail Gorbachev. Gorbachev was planning to visit London, and he was looking for ideas on how to reform the Soviet Union.

When Gorbachev arrived, guess who

acted as his offical London escort? An obscure member of parliament named John Browne, who at that time was a contributing editor to STRATEGIC INVESTMENT.

STRATEGIC INVESTMENT contacts spent a lot of time with Gorbachev and his wife. It soon became clear that Gorbachev had been picked to replace the ailing Chernenko as head of state.

It was also clear that the Gorbachevs, had the style and charisma to become "the John and Jackie Kennedy of our time." That was how STRATEGIC INVESTMENT put it back in 1985.

We learned that Gorbachev had a different approach to world politics than any previous Soviet leader. . .and that it would be a mistake to rely on the old Cold War formulas for predicting events. On the other hand, we also knew that you could make a lot of money on your investments as a result of the knowledge we had gained.

We were able to probe Gorbachev on a number of subjects and report our findings directly to STRATEGIC INVESTMENT readers. The results are on record in the January '85 issue.

A lot has happened since then—much more than most people anticipated. Almost all of the developments in world politics we predicted have come to pass. A lot of people have gotten very rich from following the investment advice that grew out of these insights.

On the other hand, others hate our guts for revealing the truth about what was going on in the world.

In fact, we were once accused of being a CIA front by the left-wing magazine *Mother Jones*.

We were flattered, in a way, but they were mistaken. Let me tell you more about our worldwide sources.

꙳

Chapter Six

How to Beat the Market with Inside Information

Soon after the '92 election, STRATEGIC INVESTMENT told readers what Clinton would do in his first 100 days.

How did we know? We didn't read it in the papers. I talked to top Clinton strategists. I visited with some of his close friends from Oxford, big campaign contributors, and members of Congress. Many of my contacts were later appointed to high posts in the White House.

I even sat down to dinner with Clinton himself. I've known him for many years, and I like to consider myself an "FOB" (Friend of Bill's), even though I don't agree with his politics.

With the information I learned from my sources, I was able to make some startling predictions in the January issue of STRATEGIC INVESTMENT. That issue was in the hands of our readers before the Inauguration. Here is what we said:

- Clinton would propose a tougher deficit reduction package than the stock market expected.

- Income taxes on the upper brackets in the U.S. would go up sharply and inheritance taxes would increase.

- Social Security spending would be cut.

- A gasoline tax would be imposed.

- Interest rates would actually go *down* in the first months of 1993. The fall in interest rates would spark a rally in stocks and bonds.

- Clinton would cut the military much more than Bush had planned (bad news for California and a host of stocks).

In short, STRATEGIC INVESTMENT had formed a better idea of what Clinton was likely to do than even some of his top aides.

Three weeks after the Inauguration, the mainstream press was still wondering, "What's going to be in Clinton's economic plan? What is he going to say in his State of the Union address?" STRATEGIC INVESTMENT readers already knew and were able to position themselves to take advantage.

As late as March, the mainstream press was still saying, "Golly, gee, interest rates are going down. Who would have thought?" Meanwhile, STRATEGIC INVESTMENT readers were able to play a major bond rally. The government's 30-year bond went up in the months following my article. (I also warned that the rally wouldn't last.)

In a moment, I'm going to tell you a vital piece of information I learned through my Oxford connection (but not directly from Bill Clinton, who would never drop this bombshell himself). This piece of information may be worth $138,000 to you. (See page 76.)

Markets Don't Move at Random

Much of our success is based on a key insight. It's illegal to profit from inside information about stocks. But there is no such problem with inside political information.

Let's face it. Markets do not move totally at random. They move because somebody decides to do something. People move markets. And powerful people move them powerfully. When stocks shoot down or up, it is usually because of actions taken in Washington, or Tokyo, or Bonn.

Wouldn't you like to know about those actions in advance?

We would. And we created the most sophisticated, high-level network in the world to bring you the information you need before it becomes common knowledge.

One of our contacts runs one of the biggest investment portfolios in London. Another is a former president of the Rothschild Bank in Zurich. Another source is the former chairman of one of the world's largest oil companies.

How do we know so much about Russia? One of our contacts is the great grandson of Czar Alexander II.

Let me tell you about some of the profit opportunities I've identified.

&

Chapter Seven _____

Turning Chaos Into Cash: Four Slam-Dunk Investments for the '90s

Lord Rees-Mogg and I called our first book *Blood in the Streets*. Its subtitle was "Investment Profits in a World Gone Mad." A lot of people thought we were overdoing it just a bit.

But consider the forecasts we made that came true:

- **The Crash of '87.**

- **The collapse in U.S. real estate values** — and the banking crisis that resulted.

- **The crash in Tokyo stocks** and real estate, with losses in the trillions. (Our readers tripled their money on the fall in Japanese stocks. . .with a low-risk investment you could buy from any U.S. broker.)

- **The end of the Soviet Union** and the Cold War. The CIA got this one wrong. The government could have saved $30 billion in "intelligence gathering" by subscribing to STRATEGIC INVEST-MENT.

- **Falling incomes** for blue collar workers and massive layoffs among middle managers.

- **Huge cutbacks in defense spending.** (We predicted this while the Reagan build-up was at its height.)

- **The fall of the Berlin Wall** and German reunification. In 1986, we gave renewing subscribers "worthless bonds" from former East German private companies and told them to wait. Our forecast came true and those dead bonds came back to life.

The "experts" laughed, but we were right. And we've continued to forecast developments that the Establishment thought would not happen.

- **The U.S. recession.** In January 1990, when the *Washington Post* was proclaiming that the business cycle might be "out of business," we said that a recession lay ahead.

- **The defeat of George Bush.** In January 1991, we told readers that George Bush would end up unconsciously imitating Herbert Hoover's speeches about prosperity being "just around the corner." In January of '92, ten months before the election, we said Clinton would be nominated and would win. The rest of the press was writing about Gennifer Flowers.

- **Government layoffs.** Two years ago, we said "unprecedented numbers of government employees would be fired in the 1990s." Now Clinton says he's going to cut 100,000 — not including military.

Our objective here at STRATEGIC INVESTMENT is to protect you from all this bad news and to help you actually grow wealthy from it. Following are four investments. They are my short list of ideal moneymakers during the coming bad years (there are many more in your monthly issues of STRATEGIC INVESTMENT).

───── **The Clinton Portfolio** ─────

#1 Ideal Investment for the Coming Bad Years

Earn 500% Profit, Government-Guaranteed!

You can buy a bond today for $13,900 that will pay you $84,000 in 2019 — $6 back for every dollar you invest. What's more, it's 100% government-guaranteed — not by the U.S. government, which is going to run away from its obligations. This bond is fully backed by the government of France, which doesn't have our debt problems and has not defaulted on a bond since they got rid of the Nazis. It may surprise you, but France is actually a better credit risk than Germany.

I have carefully chosen this French bond as my #1 Ideal Investment, even for the most conservative investor. It's as close to a can't-lose proposition as I can find in today's world.

These bonds will pay off handsomely for you even if a great depression does not occur, and they will pay you capital gains beyond your wildest dreams if it does.

This trick is possible because these are *zero-coupon* government bonds. They don't pay you interest every year — you get all the interest plus your principal in the year 2019 — six dollars then for every dollar you put up now.

Thanks to this unusual feature, you don't have to hold them to maturity to make a lot of money. You can sell them at any time. You see, zero-coupon bonds respond like crazy to even tiny changes in interest rates. If interest rates go down just 1% in France, these bonds will jump 36%. If rates go down 2%, you'll make 73%!

And I am very confident that French rates will go down. As this goes to press, their rates are among the highest in the world.

Short-term interest rates in France are 9.25% compared to less than 3% in the U.S. Yet French inflation is under 2%, about half ours. A reduction in French rates is *extremely* likely, giving you a huge gain.

But if French rates never, ever come down for the next 26 years, the worst that can happen is that you hold these bonds until they mature. You're guaranteed to earn over 7.1% per year on your money with little risk over that whole period.

Buy Them Right Here in the U.S.

You can buy the French zero strip, maturing in 10/2019, by writing Prudential Securities, 815 Connecticut Ave., NW, Ste. 300, Washington, D.C. 20006. (You may call them at 202-872-6539, but due to the response to this book, it may be hard to get through.)

If you lock in this unusually high 7.1% rate, *the least you are guaranteed to make on your money is 500%.* That's if you hold them until 2019. But what I really expect will happen is this. . .

You'll make 50% or more on your money in the next 12-24 months! As the returns on other investments fall, the value of your bonds will skyrocket. That's because you'll own something government-guaranteed to pay 7.1% for the next 26 years while other investments pay 2%, 3%, or even less.

———— The Clinton Portfolio ————

#2 Ideal Investment for the Coming Bad Years

An Easy Double

Suppose I offer you a stock that is selling for less than $4 per share but is backed by $75 per share in assets.

Suppose I tell you the company can make a profit even if the product it sells declines to half what it's worth right now.

Suppose I then tell you that the value of its assets will soar if the Clinton economy is healthy (contrary to what I expect). . .but the value will skyrocket *even more* if Clinton lets inflation get out of control.

Suppose I also reveal that there are two lenders competing for the privilege of lending this company money. And there is also a huge corp of investors who can't buy this stock now but who will jump in at the first chance.

Would you buy? I suspect you would.

The stock is a copper mining firm called *AZCO*. It's an American public company, now traded on the Toronto Stock Exchange (symbol AZC) for less than $4 Canadian.

If you like to make money, you're going to

love AZCO. It's about as close to depression-proof as you can get. If the opposite happens and inflation takes off, AZCO is going to be the best thing you can possibly hold. If we have a healthy economy — neither inflation nor depression — you could easily get a 500% return or more in the next three years.

AZCO has 100% rights in three of the world's largest copper deposits, one in Arizona and two in Mexico. $75 per share is the estimated value of these vast reserves.

What's more, AZCO extracts the copper with the most advanced technology — an environmentally friendly process that also saves up to 34 cents per pound by bypassing the smelter. Bruce Babbitt, Clinton's Secretary of the Interior, worked on AZCO's environmental impact statement. So it's extremely unlikely that the Feds are going to give AZCO a problem.

This advanced process gives AZCO a cost per pound of about 49 cents vs. 65 cents to a dollar for their competitors. With the world price of copper about 84 cents, AZCO can make money at nearly half-off. But just in case, the management has arranged with one of the world's largest banks to make sure they will not receive less than 80 cents for at least three years.

Typical of small stocks, the large institutional investors such as pension funds and mutual funds can't buy AZCO right now because it's too small. (A mutual fund is not permitted to own more than 10% of a company's stock.) A few years from now, when AZCO is one of the world's largest copper miners, these big players will jump in with both feet.

That will drive the price up even more. Don't miss out.

———— **The Clinton Portfolio** ————

#3 Ideal Investment for the Coming Bad Years

Earn a Tax-Sheltered 8.0%

Lakehead Pipeline LP (LHP-NYSE) is yielding 8.0%. Because it is a limited partnership, much of the gain is treated as tax-free return of principal — this year, about half your distribution is tax free. You won't pay taxes unless you sell your shares.

Lakehead Pipeline LP owns the 1,100-mile-long U.S. portion of the oil and gas pipeline which runs 2,300 miles from western Canada to eastern Canada.

And here's the "risk-reducer": *This is the only pipeline that transports crude oil from western to eastern Canada.* Come inflation or depression, the folks in eastern Canada will still need oil. It's a sure bet.

This one is so safe, I bought it for my mother.

There's another risk-reducer: Lakehead *guarantees* an annual $2.36 distribution through Dec. 31, 1996. There's substantial cash in the bank escrowed to cover it. That gives you 8.0%, come what may.

And finally, there's a *third* risk-reducer: The partnership has a large rate increase pending before the U.S. government. Lakehead is already collecting the money from its customers, but it is not distributing the money to limited partners until the rate increase is approved, probably in early '94.

Once approval comes through, I expect the limited partners will get a big windfall profit distribution, and thereafter the distributions should be well above the $2.36 per year that the company guarantees for now.

So at current prices on the New York Stock Exchange, I expect 8.0% per year is the *least* you're going to make.

———— **The Clinton Portfolio** ————

#4 Ideal Investment for the Coming Bad Years

Gore-Proof Your Portfolio

Bill Clinton's VP, Al Gore, believes we're

headed for global environmental catastrophe. To prevent it, he'd like to spend hundreds of billions as soon as possible.

We're already committed to spending $50 billion to plug an ozone hole that doesn't exist. (It costs $500 per car to replace the Freon in the air conditioner with something "harmless.") There's worse to come. But you can protect yourself and actually *profit* from environmental hysteria.

I believe I have found a company with a multi-billion dollar idea that is still selling for backwoods prices: Innovative Environmental Services Ltd. (Alberta; INV).

Before I tell you more, I must admit a prejudice. INV has excited me so much that I have become personally involved in the company in a direct way. Be aware as you read what I say that I stand to make a large amount of money if the stock price goes up.

INV employs computer-controlled sequencing batch reactors (CSBR) to decompose sewage and other biodegradable wastes. If this sounds boring, think again: It could be the equivalent of "biotech for land."

Just as biotech companies like Synergen have engineered new drugs that have vast potential markets, Innovative Environmental Systems has a technology that can increase land values in a dramatic way. It can turn costs into profits for city governments, reduce pressure for higher taxes, and clean up all kinds of waste sites.

Unless I am very wrong, INV should be a spectacular stock for the 1990s. It stands to benefit from a number of powerful trends that Lord Rees-Mogg and I highlighted in our best-seller *The Great Reckoning*, including bankruptcy of local governments, privatization, and worries about the environment.

INV can offer immediate budget relief to bankrupt local governments by turning sewage systems into private, for-profit companies. It eliminates the need for these governments to invest billions in sewage capacity.

INV's high-tech treatment system converts effluent into water that can be used for irrigation and power generation. From chicken farms to lumber mills, it has applications for treating troublesome industrial wastes.

The system can raise the value of out-of-the-way rural property that can't be developed now because of waste disposal and clean-up problems. It opens the way to develop lake-front and ocean-front resort land that is currently off limits.

Granted, the stock is small and speculative, but if it can tap even a bare trace of its potential, it won't be a small company for long.

❧

Chapter Eight _____

It Takes More Than Friends in High Places

All the high-level contacts in the world are useless unless you understand what to do with the information. There are hundreds of writers and journalists with friends in high places, but most of what they write is dead wrong. They just don't get it.

At STRATEGIC INVESTMENT, our track record pretty well proves we "get it." Our secret is the theory of Megapolitics.

Now, that's a concept Lord Rees-Mogg and I invented. We explained it at length in our two best-selling books *Blood in the Streets* (1987) and *The Great Reckoning* (1991).

You don't have to read those books to understand the main idea: The world is shaped by big, powerful forces or trends that nobody can control. In fact, very few people are even aware of them. There are historical cycles that repeat themselves over and over. There have been nine depressions, spaced about 60 years apart, since the mid-16th century.

One explanation for this is human psychology. After a depression, the generation that suffered through it is very careful and conservative. Lenders make only totally-safe, no-risk loans. Investors will invest only in sure things. It was 1954 before the Dow Jones Industrial Average reached the level it had attained in the boom of the 1920s.

Then, about 30 or 40 years after a depression, a new generation begins to take over. Its members have little memory of the crash. They think their elders are over-cautious old fuddie-duddies who are missing profit opportunities. And, in a way, the young people are right. It's time to be more aggressive. Think of the 1950s and 1960s.

As this new generation takes control of banks, corporations, government and other institutions, caution is eventually thrown to the winds. By about 60 years after the last crash, there's almost no one around who remembers what it was like. Stocks and real estate have gone up for as long as these people can remember.

The stage is set for another depression, caused by the cheap money, bad loans and foolish investments of the boom generation. That's where we are now. The "credit cycle" began to unwind in 1987, but it still has a long way to go. The worst is yet to come.

The 500-Year Cycle

There is also a long 500-year cycle. No

one knows precisely why this is. I believe we will eventually uncover a scientific explanation.

But I do know that the cycle is unusually precise. Between 50 B.C. and 50 A.D. the Christian religion began and the Roman Republic was replaced by an empire. Around 500 A.D. the Roman Empire collapsed. About 1000 A.D. the Dark Ages gave way to the Middle Ages. And around 1500 A.D. the Modern Age — our age — began. In the Appendix on page 103, I've described the cycles in greater detail.

> We are now at the turning points of both the 60-year and the 500-year cycles. If history is any guide, this will be a period of war, depression, dramatic changes in techonolgy, and vast upheaval.

All turns in the 60-year cycle follow a period of excessive debt. All involve a credit crisis, all lead to a collapse of property values, all ruin independent businessmen, all have serious political consequences, and all cause high unemployment and social distress.

> Strange repetitions have occurred. The 1929 and 1987 crashes both took place on Mondays in October. In the third week of September, 1931, Brit-

ain went off the Gold Standard. In the same week in 1992, Britain left the European Exchange Rate Mechanism (ERM). Its action set off the worst currency crisis in Europe since the '30s. Interest rates in Sweden went to 500%!

This isn't idle chitchat. There are opportunities to make enormous amounts of money. In July, 1992, Prime Minister John Major was telling everyone including his wife that he would not devalue the pound. In our July issue, we wrote, "Devaluation of sterling. . .is likely within the next two months."

It happened. That one paragraph would have made you $25,000 on an investment of $4,050.

We were able to make this call because we looked for and found vital inside information about the intense pressures building in Britain. *And* because we're aware of the big cycles and we factor them into our strategy.

Each of the great 60-year turning points creates a whole new class of millionaires and wipes out the accumulated wealth of the old class. New technologies wipe out mistaken investments in old technologies (IBM and mainframes, for example).

Society has to write off debts that were piled up too high when times were good. Government can shuffle the pain around — another reason to have inside political information. But government cannot *escape* the pain.

The Market Is More Powerful Than Any Government

The biggest mistake of our time is the belief that government *can* avoid the cost of bad debts and outmoded investments. Just as the Russians found out you can't create a society in which no one can make a profit, we're going to find out you can't have a society in which no one takes a loss.

The Democrats have set off on a policy of rescuing old, mature industries and big unions. It's not going to work. Out of the depression of the '30s, a group of key new industries emerged: jet aircraft, television, guided missiles, and mainframe computers. Those industries were the foundation of the postwar years, but now they have run their course. Trying to resurrect industrial America, as Clinton wants to, will actually make things worse. It will merely pile up more debt.

From These Cycles Come Profit. . .And Peril

As we enter into a new era, Marxism and Communism have already been discredited.

Only a few backward countries and American universities still worship their false prophets. But I bet you'll be surprised by another development: the extinction of capitalism. Yes, capitalism as we know it will soon disappear.

Oh, the word will still be bandied about in the same way that "industrial" is. But society is fast reorganizing around people who can increase productivity and innovation through information or *knowledge*.

Knowledge is the new nucleus, the resource of highest value, replacing capital, labor, and materials as the raw components of progress in a new Information Era. Manufacturing and trade will continue, of course, but the people who carry the knowledge will carry the day.

For confirmation, take one look at Bill Gates, the boyish chairman of Microsoft who just started shaving recently. Gates makes software for computers, and he's the richest fellow in America. Worth billions!

It's no coincidence.

When major historical changes are in motion, you want to be one of the first to understand. You want to invest with the positive trends and get out of the way of the negative trends. And you can do so with the advance information you'll receive from STRATEGIC INVESTMENT.

The nine-letter key to wealth is KNOWL-EDGE. It equals power in the new era. That's why STRATEGIC INVESTMENT is such a valuable resource. You can use the advance knowledge we provide to gain power, to gain money, to gain whatever you please.

But it's urgent that you take action now.

A lot of people's plans are going to be upset—including the plans of one very famous American. Turn to the next chapter to see what I mean.

&

Chapter Nine _____

The Story of a One-Term President

Once upon a time, there was a presidential election in the United States. A few months after the election, the uninspiring man from New England left the White House. The press wasn't sorry to see him go. The departing President disliked the hustling newcomer and called him the "Wonder Boy."

But most of the nation hailed the dynamic, youthful new President from the nation's heartland. Some called him the most brilliant man who had ever become President. His achievements were even more amazing because he came from a poor background and never knew his real father.

The new President was keen on high technology. He believed that planning and analysis could solve the nation's problems much as you would solve an engineering problem. A Philadelphia newspaper called him "easily the most commanding figure in the modern science of 'engineering statesmanship.'"

Wherever he went he created a great buzz. He formed committees and trade councils, sponsored research programs, boosted funding, commissioned reports, and created working groups to tackle problems.

Unlike his "do-nothing" predecessors, he was a "policy wonk" who often knew the details of an issue better than the experts. Education, the oil industry, medical care for children, conservation — he was intensely interested in every public issue. He often took a personal hand in drafting bills.

The new President's basic idea was simple: If business, labor, and government would just work together life would constantly become better.

Fighting the Downturn

Faced with an economic downturn that wasn't his fault, the President boldly used all the resources of government to turn it around.

Low interest rates were the cornerstone of his policy. The Federal Reserve poured money into the economy. The government got "tough on trade" and moved to keep out unfair foreign competition.

Huge stimulus programs were passed. More major public works were started in his four years than in the previous 30. He leaned on business to hire more people and to avoid wage cuts. Loans and grants flew out to needy and distressed groups as fast as the

President could sign the bills.

Alas, everyone agreed that something had to be done about runaway budget deficits. He signed the biggest peacetime tax increase in U.S. history. The top rate jumped from 25% to 63%.

It was all in vain. The downturn deepened into the biggest depression ever. Washington's streets filled with protesters demanding money from the government. The President had to use the Army to clear them out.

Four years after sweeping into the Oval Office on a wave of hope, the President was buried in a landslide. Strangest of all, historians would blame him for not doing enough to stop the economic collapse.

Bill Clinton four years from now? No. The man was Herbert Hoover, President from 1929-33 and scapegoat for the Great Depression.

I tell you this little story not to be clever but to make an important point. History repeats itself, often in startling ways.

I'm not a foe of Bill Clinton's. As I mentioned earlier, I've known him for many years and I consider myself an "FOB" (Friend of

Bill's). I do happen to think he is a brilliant man.

But friendship aside, I have a prediction that might startle you during this Bill Clinton "honeymoon": The marriage is already headed for the rocks.

> Bill Clinton is going to be a one-term President. He's going to get clobbered in the '96 election, assuming his own party even renominates him. I'm as sure of this as I am that the sun will rise tomorrow.

Bill Clinton's failure will take place against a background of deep depression, urban riots, and people losing their homes. The Los Angeles riots and the bomb at New York's World Trade Center are a small taste of what's to come.

I can say this with authority because I predicted these two events and many others. To most people the news is just a jumble of events that doesn't make any sense. They don't see a connection between the Branch Davidians in Texas and the war in Bosnia, for example.

But there are connections. These things don't happen at random. You can know what's coming. . . and enjoy a big edge over other investors. . . besides protecting your property, your life, and the lives of your loved ones.

When the crisis erupts, Bill Clinton is
going to take drastic steps to save his
presidency. This book is a "sneak
preview" of what those steps are going
to be. It's urgent that you take action
at once.

You can also profit if you know that
California, New York City and other states
and cities will go broke on a grand scale. Yes,
you've already heard about these problems.
But what we've seen so far is just an omen.

The bankruptcies to come will change
the landscape for fifty years. Services will be
cut to nothing. Decay will accelerate. Millions
of businesses and citizens will leave these
states for good.

The problems won't be confined to the
U.S. And they won't be just economic.

Let me show you what I mean. . .

&

Third World Nukes

It surprised some people back in '87 when we said the Soviet Union would not only collapse but its collapse might *not* be good news. We said that a world without the Soviet Union could be a bigger threat to peace and prosperity than the Reds ever were.

Now Russia is in upheaval, Christians battle Muslims in Yugoslavia, and our critics are starting to get the message. We also pointed out that individual Soviet republics like Ukraine and Kazakhstan are now nuclear powers.

Our intelligence sources now tell us Iran has acquired two 40-kiloton nuclear devices from Kazakhstan. They can be dropped from aircraft, and Iran is working day and night to develop intermediate-range delivery missiles.

The Rise of Islam

Here in North America it is hard to imagine people willing to fight (and die) for religion. Religious wars seem like a relic of the past. This is an age of materialism. People are much more interested in the prospect of profit than the promise of heaven.

But this is not true everywhere. Especially troubling for many in the West will be the rise of Islam. Muslim populations in the former Soviet Union are breaking away. . . and they are not forming democracies.

Chances are, their huge weapons arsenals and vast populations will be aligned with Iraq, Iran and the rest of the militant Islamic world. *This could be the biggest threat to world peace in the next two decades.*

As our experience with Saddam Hussein demonstrates, these people have a much different idea of government and individual rights than we have. Many Islamic fundamentalists regard the West as weak and decadent. You and I are enemies of God — literally. "Great Satan" was how Khomeini referred to America. And he spoke for millions of other Muslims.

There's a profit angle here, too. While defense spending in general is cut in the U.S., there are a couple of companies that stand to make a mint with their anti-terrorist devices.

Just as communism welded together the parts of the Soviet Empire and turned them into a powerful and dangerous force, Islam might soon do the same thing — unifying a region as large as the Soviet Union and with millions more people.

It wouldn't be the first time in history that Islam has gone to war with the West. But it might be the last. This new Pan-Islamic Federation might have little respect for Western institutions, but it will certainly have one Western legacy — nuclear weapons — thanks to the Soviet break-up.

The rise of Islam and the spread of nuclear weapons is just one part of the most important trend in the world. To learn more, keep reading.

ઢ

The Most Important World Trend

While others gloated over the Cold War "victory," here at STRATEGIC INVEST-MENT we saw an era of trouble on the horizon. Like it or not, the Soviets were dependable. Almost conservative.

Since the end of World War II they suppressed a lot of local conflicts. They kept things under control. And they provided an indirect bonus to a lot of Americans. That "Soviet subsidy" is about to end.

I've had an unusual vantage point on these developments. A couple of years ago I was appointed Advisor on Economic Reform to the Republic of Belarus, once part of the Soviet Union. It amounts to the first time in history that an entire nation has become a subscriber to an investment newsletter.

Officials in Belarus told me that tactical nuclear weapons formerly stationed there had been removed, adding, "But we can't be sure where they went. For all we know, Saddam Hussein has them."

Frankly, I expect things to get danger-ously out of control in the next few years. *The most important worldwide trend is that the large, wealthy countries can no longer control small countries.*

This is obvious when you look at the break-up of the Soviet Union. Maybe you don't think it's obvious here in the United States. But in fact we can't control our own cities or our own borders. Does the U.S. "control" south central Los Angeles any more than Russia controls Latvia? Of course not. A Russian is a great deal safer in Latvia than you are in L.A.

Here's what *USA Today* offered in its February 15 issue. They interviewed some of L.A.'s 80,000 gang members:

> "The gangs are heavily armed. It's hard to find anyone who doesn't own at least one gun — especially after the looting of gun and army surplus stores during last year's riots, and a 30% rise in gun store thefts since then. . .

> "Stung by criticism that they trashed their own neighborhoods last year, gang members say they'll do it differently this time. If there's burning, they'll do it outside their own neighborhoods, jetting up the long avenues that run into Koreatown and predominantly white neighborhoods."

The principal gangs — the Crips and the Bloods — have spread to cities all over the nation. They are heavily involved in the drug trade. A gang member interviewed on Dallas radio told listeners that "next time" the action will be carried to Highland Park, the city's wealthiest enclave.

A New Wave of Terrorism

Our second book, *The Great Reckoning*, predicted urban riots would return to the United States. Urban violence is a natural outgrowth of the end of the American way of life — a symptom of the collapse of the old order.

The '92 riots in Los Angeles erupted only months after the book hit the stands. We also predicted a new wave of terrorism. Along came the bomb in New York's World Trade Center.

Here's what Lord Rees-Mogg and I said in *The Great Reckoning*, published August, 1991:

> "New York is highly vulnerable to sabotage, terrorism, and simple infrastructure breakdown. . .Tunnels, bridges, pumping stations, and powerlines, are all practically unguarded. Many could not be guarded. . . The wonder is that

some terrorist group or a criminal gang has not already held the city for ransom by sabotaging crucial facilities."

The World Trade Center bomb was homemade with materials you or I could buy off the shelf. It was created by freelance terrorists, not people directed by Moscow or Baghdad.

The bombers came within an ace of shutting down important financial markets. The bomb would have brought down a smaller skyscraper.

Tony Cooper is a specialist who monitors terrorist activity. Asked why there haven't been more fatal attacks, he said, "The only reason that hasn't been done is because nobody wanted to do it. We have simply been overconfident. We have taken the view that this kind of thing doesn't happen here."

1.9 million AK-47 automatic rifles were imported from China to the U.S. between 1989 and 1991 alone. This favorite weapon of terrorists and guerillas is now as common as VW Beetles were during the '60s, and will be coming soon to your neighborhood.

Two thousand bombings were reported to the FBI in 1991, up 58 percent from the year before. Why don't we hear about this? Because the mainstream press doesn't want people to get "alarmed." You don't learn about it until the world's tallest buildings are almost blown up — *unless* you read STRATEGIC INVESTMENT. (To help you get started, I'd like to send you a free copy of our hardcover book, *The Great Reckoning*, when you subscribe. See page 115.)

The Secret Connections Between Events

From Bosnia to the Branch Davidians in Texas, these events are all connected in a way that Dan Rather and CNN can't explain, but the theory of Megapolitics *can*.

We live at the turning point of a 60-year "long wave" cycle. These turning points are not only signaled by economic troubles, but also by *new technologies that alter the balance of power*. The new technologies in play now are small computers and cheap, handheld weapons. The cost of both has come down to virtually nothing, giving "power to the people" — that dream of '60s radicals.

Both of these technologies make it almost impossible for powerful central governments to remain in control. That's why big governments from Russia to India to Canada are breaking apart, and that's why America can't control its own cities. It's also why Clinton's get-the-rich policies will be a miserable flop.

Unlike a steel mill, politicians can't hold

a computer program hostage to their demands. A steel mill can scarcely be moved when legislators determine to tax it or to regulate its owners. But a computer program can be transmitted by modem at the speed of light anywhere in the world. The owner can pack his 486 laptop and fly away. The rich aren't going to hang around to be ripped off.

These dramatic changes in technology are taking place just when governments can least afford it. The present situation is like a pile of gasoline-soaked rags waiting for a match. The coming economic collapse will be the match.

We are overdue for a massive economic downturn. The train is so late a good many people have convinced themselves it's never going to arrive. "This time it's different," they tell themselves.

Don't count on it. Read my monthly report, *Strategic Investment*. Then you'll know about the train before it comes roaring down on top of you.

The last 50 years were one of the longest periods of stability in history. You only have to read your newspaper to see that this period is coming to an end.

Our job is to tell you what the papers will

be saying a year from now. . .five years from now. Look for wars. . .border disputes. . . bitter racial and ethnic conflict. . . terrorism . . .and urban riots.

What good is this information? Believe me, here at STRATEGIC INVESTMENT we're bottom-line oriented. There are few far-reaching world events you can't make a profit on. Cases in point:

June 1991: Our cover story warned specifically that there would be a coup against Gorbachev. We told you what to expect when the attempt was made: "The dollar will rise and stock markets generally will suffer, with the German market most vulnerable. . .You should use any temporary strength in defense stocks following a shift in Gorbachev's status as a selling opportunity."

When the attempted military coup did occur two months after our cover story, the trading advice proved absolutely accurate.

February 1993: We said, "The situation is so weak that the Japanese government is intent on ramping [running up] the market before the close of the fiscal year in March. . ." Bingo! The market soared 25% in the next nine weeks. Even the mainstream press admits it was entirely due to government manipulation.

How can you make a profit on the coming Middle East war? The best device is a simple, low-risk way that we describe fully in our FREE report *The Clinton Years*. It allows you to make about $5,000 in profit for every $1,000 you put up. And it's as simple as calling a broker.

The key is timing. And we'll give you that in the pages of STRATEGIC INVESTMENT newsletter.

The point is this: You can be among the few people who foresee and profit from major developments.

It doesn't take a crystal ball. All that is required is the right contacts, information, and an understanding of economic and political links between events.

And that has been the hallmark of STRATEGIC INVESTMENT from the very beginning. STRATEGIC INVESTMENT is living proof that you can know. . .you can understand. . .and you can profit from the seemingly chaotic markets around you.

ॐ

Chapter Twelve _____

How Will Clinton Try to Salvage His Presidency?

My friend Bill Clinton is facing an Economic Dunkirk. There is no better analogy. He will be bombarded on all sides by a crushing national debt, falling output, rising unemployment and social unrest. He won't just sit there. He's going to try to do something.

I can tell you what he will try to do.

At the rate the $4 trillion debt is expanding, the interest payments alone will consume 100% of income tax payments in just 3-4 years. The government's whole operating budget, besides interest, will have to be borrowed.

Obviously, Clinton can't let that happen. So what will he do? Will he stand tall or blink? Here's the worst-case scenario:

Clinton will raise taxes far above the 39.6% level (actually, 44%) he's already signed into law. (How do I know this? Keep reading.) Clinton will also be forced to slash Social Security, Medicare, Medicaid, and farm subsidies. He'll fire legions of government employees. There will be few sacred cows left because there won't be enough money to pay for the hay.

That's the worst-case scenario. For the best case, reread the last paragraph.

But wait, you say, why wouldn't Clinton simply inflate his way out of the economic wreckage he inherited? That's what governments usually do when faced with economic problems. A lot of newsletter writers are predicting that Clinton will crank open the money spigots in hopes of inflating away his problems.

But the thing you have to understand about most financial advisors is that, like most generals, they are always fighting the last war. The fact is, the inflation option is no longer available to Clinton.

Bond Traders Now Veto Presidents

Bond traders aren't elected, and they answer to nobody. But they possess *knowledge* about market prices around the world. In the new Information Era, they can move trillions of dollars at the speed of light. And that makes them very powerful.

At the first inkling that Bill Clinton is

trying to reflate the economy by pumping
funny money into it, thousands of bond traders will dump hundreds of billions of dollars
in U.S. bonds. Interest rates will shoot up
like an Apollo booster: slowly at first, then
with unbelievable power and speed.

The government debt is almost all short
term and has to be refinanced every year or
two. With 20% interest rates — and remember, we had them in 1980 — the interest on
the national debt would be *five times* what it
is now. It would be greater than all the rest of
the budget combined. *It would take one dollar out of every five earned by every man,
woman and child in the United States just to
pay the interest on the debt.* And there wouldn't
be a penny of tax money left for anything else,
from Social Security to the military to the
Weather Service.

It would take an Argentina-scale inflation to get out of this. The government
wouldn't be able to borrow again for a generation. The value of money would be totally
destroyed, and with it most of the middle
class.

Every major government that ever tried
the inflation option ended up falling from
power, usually in bloody revolutions. Clinton
knows this. It's not going to happen.

So what *will* Clinton do to bail himself
out of a seemingly impossible situation?

The Plan to Take $138,000 of Your Money

Yes, $138,000. And that's just *one* installment, as I'll explain in a moment. Do you know how to protect yourself?

What Mr. Clinton *wants* to do in office and what he'll be *forced* to do are two very different things.

Clinton tells us he'll make government work by "tapping the kind of idealism that really hasn't been tapped since the early days of the Kennedy administration." Right. The '90s are not the '60s and Clinton does not live in Camelot.

Then Clinton tells us he's "solved" the debt problem by raising $200 billion in new revenue from "the rich." That still leaves the Treasury flat broke in three or four years.

So, after all the shouting, the question is still there: What will Clinton do when he finds the interest payments on the debt swallowing up the whole federal pie?

The Oxford Connection

Last year, before Bill Clinton was even elected, I knew it was urgent to get an answer to that question, so I could advise our readers on how to act. To get this valuable information, I turned to STRATEGIC INVESTMENT's intelligence network.

Bill Clinton may talk like a good ole boy, but he's an alumnus of Georgetown and Oxford, where he met a man named Robert Reich. The two had a profound impact on each other. It was no surprise that Clinton tapped Reich, a Harvard prof, to help him make sense of the economy.

As I mentioned earlier, I attended Oxford. So did Lord Rees-Mogg. Two members of our intelligence network attended Georgetown, a training camp for Washington insiders. If you want to know what's cooking in Bill Clinton's head, you'd better tap into *this* old boy network, not the good ole boys in Arkansas.

The Oxford Connection holds the clue to what Bill Clinton will do about the economic crisis. And it's truly frightening.

I've concluded that Clinton will raise taxes even more. *This is a sure bet*. When cornered, raising taxes will be the easiest thing for Clinton to do.

You see, Robert Reich is a firm believer in economic planning. He has little respect for the private economy or for entrepreneurs — he thinks "teams" do everything now. And he plans for government to be the captain of the team. What's more, he wants to turn back the clock to the days of big industrial corporations and powerful unions.

Reich has already taken steps to make it easier for unions to strike. He also wants to re-unionize the private sector, where almost no one belongs to labor unions anymore.

Basically, he thinks the economy is slow because the government doesn't do enough. He thinks the private sector is *too big* and has *too much power*.

He's been called "the Karl Marx of the Information Age."

It's not a fluke that he's in the Clinton cabinet. He has plenty of company there, including Donna Shalala and Hillary Rodham Clinton. It is already clear that Mr. Clinton is no "new Democrat."

Clinton's tax increase leaves him well-shy of what's needed to pay the bills. He'll be back asking for additional tax increases. And with the help of a Democratic Congress, he'll get them. Bob Reich and other top advisors will be there with the academic mumbo-jumbo to justify it all.

In 1994 or the year after, Clinton will go on nationwide TV. He'll look us right in the eyes. And he'll tell us that his program to raise the tax brackets to 36% for people earning over $115,000 has been so successful, that he's raising the rate to 50% and lowering the income level to $60,000!

But That's Not All!

Besides raising tax brackets, Clinton will raise a host of other new taxes, great and small. Remember, Clinton will be slashing Social Security, Medicare and every other type of government spending. The victims of these cuts are going to be in a rage. They're going to be baying for blood.

And Clinton will give them somebody's blood: yours.

Ladies and gentleman, this is not news. We've already seen Clinton's strategy is to blame the rich. But the first tax increase — and the get-the-rich rhetoric that went along with it — is just a rehearsal.

When cornered, Clinton will attack the easiest tax target — estate taxes. *You can count on it*. Why should anyone *inherit* wealth, Bob Reich is going to ask. Maybe the parents earned it, but *the kids* didn't. Tax it away! Fairness!

Clinton will cut the estate tax exemption from $600,000 all the way down to $200,000. That means your heirs will get taxed at the top rate for all but $200,000 of your estate.

If you're worth $400,000...which is easy, with a home and a few stocks. . .then your heirs will be paying $67,000 in new taxes. If you're worth $600,000 or more, your new taxes shoot up to $138,000!

Disinherit The IRS

Is there any salvation from these outrageous new taxes?

You bet! There are specific steps you can take right now to disinherit Mr. Clinton's IRS. But if you procrastinate a few months, you could lose big.

The newspapers will tell you that there's not much you can do to hold onto your money. They are foolishly naive. You can rearrange your assets to avoid the new estate taxes.

And you can avoid the higher income tax brackets by redeploying your assets into selected capital gain investments. The assets I have in mind will go up in value year after year — but you won't pay a penny in taxes on them unless you sell them.

Trillions of dollars can easily be salted away out of the government's reach. . ."buried" in capital gain assets for decades, if need be. When Ronald Reagan *lowered* capital gains taxes, he found that tax collections went *up*, as the rich cashed in their capital gains! Billions of dollars of hidden wealth came out of the woodwork.

Now it's time to bury that wealth again. This buried capital gain treasure will see you through the coming bad years. It will also be the foundation for our country to rebuild after Bill Clinton is gone in 1997.

But if you want to make capital gains, you have to purchase assets that will go up in value. Choosing which assets to buy is the whole point of STRATEGIC INVESTMENT! Not everything is going to appreciate. In fact, most assets are going to go *down* in value. Our whole reason for publishing STRATEGIC INVESTMENT is to tell you what's going *up* — and what to avoid!

Every month, STRATEGIC INVESTMENT will be your pilot, navigating you through the treacherous seas of soaring taxes and plunging stocks, bonds and real estate.

In a special report called *The $138,000 Estate Tax Surprise*, we outline the specific, 100% legal tax and investment moves you can make right now to keep more of your wealth in the family. I want to send you this special report — FREE — when you agree to try STRATEGIC INVESTMENT for one year.

જ્ર

(Publisher's Note: Due to intense outrage over these expected taxes. . .and the need to counter them quickly. . .we are accepting subscription orders by fax. See page 115.)

Chapter Thirteen _____

Professional Forecasting vs. Crystal Ball Gazing

STRATEGIC INVESTMENT has predicted the major events of our day, events that have moved markets and made enormous wealth for our readers. Every month, we update our forecasts and offer specific investment recommendations that will keep your money safe into the 21st century.

Our readers benefit from the proven, inside information of our intelligence network including updates from Lord Rees-Mogg in London, Marc Faber in Hong Kong, Michael Belkin on Wall Street, and others. You will find our forecasts to be very different from the hit-or-miss predictions of most financial advisors.

This is because our forecasts are linked to the fundamental causes of market events. . .and confirmed by sensitive, high-level intelligence you will not find in any other publication. Let me pass along a story to illustrate how useful good contacts can be.

Back in the fall of 1985, oil prices were in the upper twenties. It seemed like the oil sheiks were meeting almost every week in an effort to keep prices up. But it was obvious to everyone that OPEC's grip was getting weaker. As oil prices started to fall, our sources in Saudi Arabia informed us of a complete change in Saudi oil strategy.

We confirmed it by going to the one man who would actually decide the price of oil. In a secret interview with Sheik Yamani, who set oil prices for Saudi Arabia, we found out about the Saudi plan to do a 180-degree turnabout and drive down oil prices. The idea was to pull the rug out from under non-OPEC producers such as Norway. We reported this to our readers six months before it was headline news in *The Wall Street Journal*.

The strategy cost Yamani his job. But it also created a great profit opportunity. In a matter of weeks, the price of oil fell by half. STRATEGIC INVESTMENT predicted that the price of oil would fall below $10 by Easter '86. It did so on the day after Easter! Readers were able to make an average profit of as much as 900% on each oil contract. Pyramiding gains would have meant profits of hundreds of thousands of dollars from an original investment of just a couple thousand bucks.

That's just one example. Readers have made a fortune following our advice, often hundreds of times the subscription price.

Now the world is on the cusp of more

important changes than any we've described before. More important, even, than the collapse of the Soviet Union. In the next eighteen months, more money will be made — and lost — than ever before in world history.

You'll read about some of the new "can't miss" investments in *The Clinton Years* special report.

Investments that Fit Your Special Requirements

Each monthly issue of STRATEGIC INVESTMENT gives you specific recommendations on what to buy and sell and when. You get four carefully constructed portfolios that are sure to match you needs:

1. **Income Portfolio**. . .offers you double digit returns in a single digit world. Best of all, you enjoy these heavenly yields without being exposed to hellish risks. There's a British bond that pays 11.5%. . . a foreign utility bond that yields 18%. . .a short-term fund with a 9% yield and checkwriting privileges. You'll find them all in our Income Portfolio.

2. **Undiscovered Value** stocks are growth stocks that have not yet been recognized by Wall Street. These are usually low-priced shares of small companies with strong balance sheets. An example: We recom-

mended Heritage at $12.50 and sold at $33.25 for a gain of 166%. In fact, the entire portfolio was up more than 80% in 1989, 40% in 1990, and 35.3% in 1991, though it suffered in the down market of 1992. For years it has consistently outperformed every one of the more than 2,000 mutual funds followed by the Lipper survey.

3. **Speculative Strategy** gives you high-risk plays in commodities, currencies, options and short sales. If you want big profits, fast, the Speculative Strategy gives you a way to get them. Thanks to unconventional sources of information, our intelligence network has a remarkable success record on these exciting, high-flying investments.

4. **Blood in the Streets** is a special feature of STRATEGIC INVESTMENT. It gives you a chance to parlay the insights and information into a fortune. For example, we recommended a company selling for just 19 cents a share — with a price-earnings ratio of 1:1. The risk was minimal. The potential profits were staggering, and the portfolio itself rose 77% in 1987, a year when most investors took crippling losses.

Month after month, each issue of STRATEGIC INVESTMENT is packed with information not found anywhere else. Not in your newspaper. Not on television.

Not anywhere.

The fact is, most financial advisors know nothing about this information. They advise you to buy coins, for example, often because they sell coins! Or they urge you to buy stocks because a line on a graph seems to be heading up. Or they get scared by Wall Street gossip and tell you to sell your stocks.

But STRATEGIC INVESTMENT has no products to push or bones to pick. We are interested in only two things: Getting to the best knowledge before anyone else. . .and turning it to our profit — and yours.

It's true that many people do read STRATEGIC INVESTMENT just to know what's going on in the world. But it is designed for serious investors. Our intelligence network brings you behind-the-scenes reporting of major international events, not for the entertainment value alone. . .but because you can make money.

For Serious Investors

STRATEGIC INVESTMENT is a monthly newsletter which is chock full of money-making knowledge. Not just a rehash of what you read in *The Wall Street Journal*, but new knowledge coming from sources around the globe.

STRATEGIC INVESTMENT is clear and understandable. It's just like having a conversation with a good friend (a very well-informed friend). It also doesn't take much time. Most of the opportunities and trends are fairly long term. You don't have to follow the markets every waking hour to benefit.

You get "advance warning" of major political and economic events — and you learn how to transform those events into personal profit opportunities.

Here's My Full Offer

I'd like to send you — at no extra charge — five exclusive reports that fill you in on the details of the topics I've discussed. You'll find the knowledge you need. In addition, you'll find specific profit recommendations that will help you take advantage of your insights right away.

What's more, you will also receive a 12-month introductory subscription to STRATEGIC INVESTMENT for just $59 (regularly $109).

Of course this offer is fully guaranteed. If you decide to cancel before your fourth monthly issue, let us know and we'll return the entire amount of your subscription, promptly. No need to return the reports. . .they're yours to keep, even if you decide to cancel. If you cancel after four or more issues, we'll send a prorated refund for all unmailed issues.

But I urge you, don't delay. The economic signals are extremely dangerous. I actually hope I'm wrong, that the deficits are as harmless as some people claim. . .that the terrible tax increases and bear markets won't materialize. But I wouldn't bet on it — and neither should you.

Remember, if the special reports and your first issue of STRATEGIC INVESTMENT don't give you a taste for more. . .just cancel. It won't cost you a cent. On the other hand, if you fail to take a look at this information, and guess wrong about the market as a result, you could lose a lot.

There is a long lead time involved in publishing a book like this, and market conditions often change overnight. You should not purchase specific investments based on this report but base them on the regular, monthly issues of STRATEGIC INVESTMENT newsletter.

James Dale Davidson
August, 1993

&

An Amazing Record

Here's a sample of some of the accurate forecasts we've made in past issues of STRATEGIC INVESTMENT:

Sterling Profits (7/92)
SI wrote, "Devaluation of sterling is likely. . . within the next two months." So when England devalued on September 11, *SI* subscribers had an opportunity to pocket profits of $25,000 or more on an investment of $4,050 — a 617% gain.

Brazilian Treasure (1/91)
SI wrote: "Brazilian shares are selling at half their asset values." We recommended the Brazil Fund. Fifteen months later the fund was up 160%.

Gulf War Genie? (1/91)
While the experts were saying the Gulf War would be long and ugly, *SI* wrote, "It will be short: the greatest amount of violence in the shortest amount of time in the history of warfare." Bingo! How did *SI* know? See page 98 for an intriguing source of intelligence.

Tokyo Crash (7/90)

"How will the speculative boom in Asian equity prices end? Most stock markets in Asia are likely to fall by at least 50%." That's what *SI* wrote only weeks before the plunge began. A month later, *SI* recommended Nikkei put warrants, which gained a stunning 324%.

Soviet Disgrace (6/87)

SI predicted the Soviet disengagement from Afghanistan. Six months later, the headline of the January 7, 1988 *New York Times* read: "Moscow Declares Its Aim to Leave Afghanistan."

Argentine Treasure (12/88)

Our headline read: "Argentina: Treasure Among Depressed Markets." We said stocks were worth five times their cost. One year later Argentine shares had tripled.

Unreal Estate (10/85)

SI warned: "Don't buy real estate," and laid out a specific strategy to help you protect the value of your home and profit from the decline. The last half of the decade saw real estate values fall in most parts of North America.

Black Monday (1/86)

SI said, "If the [stock market boom] survives into '87 there is a real threat that investors will be caught in a '29 style collapse." And in January '87 *SI* urged readers to make their money early in the year. 1986 and the first half of 1987 saw spectacular profits in the stock market. By August *SI* said, "The causes of 1929 are present." On October 12, *SI* asked, "What about the Big Crash?" Five days later, one of the biggest crashes in stock market history occurred.

Oil Troubles (9/85)

SI said that oil prices are about to plunge. "Go short February crude. It looks ripe for a fall at the November 1st close of $28.60." It did — for a gain of $9,010 per contract — a profit of over 900%.

Bush Recession (1/90)

The Washington Post proclaimed, "After seven straight years of growth, maybe the business cycle is out of business." We said that a recession was ahead.

☙

Appendix Two _____

Meet the Members of Our Intelligence Network
—Steve Newby—

> "Maybe the *USA Today*/FNN National Investment Challenge should be called the Steve Newby Investment Challenge."
> —*USA Today*
> April 3, 1991

Strategic Investment contributing editor Steve Newby picked a $25,000 special portfolio in 1988 that outperformed 98% of the more than 2,300 mutual funds tracked by Lipper Analytical Services. In 1989 and 1990, it beat them all.

For the past two years he has outscored all investment advisors in the *Washingtonian* annual survey.

Recently he won the *USA Today*/Financial News Network National Investment Challenge by turning $500,000 into $1,498,763 in just 12 weeks — with the best portfolio in America.

Then, amazingly, he turned around and won the contest a second and third time —

the first investor in history to do so. He also won the 1990 *Barron's* Investment Championship, with a 272% gain in one year.

Newby has a special technique for finding undiscovered values. He invests in little known local OTC and ASE stocks. He attends dozens of stockholder meetings and monitors thousands of annual and quarterly reports. He is constantly looking for stocks not generally followed by other analysts. He then gets to know each company intimately. This hands-on research has paid off in spades.

Newby shares these profit-making opportunities with readers of *Strategic Investment*.

Our Swiss Banker in Hong Kong Who Prefers Latin America —Dr. Marc Faber—

"Marc Faber, the original bear on Japan, is no stranger to the pages of *Barron's*. He has his own investment firm, based in Hong Kong, commands both a scholarly and practical knowledge of markets around the globe, and in recent years has been particularly adept at discovering so-called emerging markets way ahead of the crowd."

—*Barron's*, April 6, 1992

Talk about a globetrotter! One of our regular *Strategic Investment* columnists, Dr. Marc Faber, was born and educated in Switzerland. He cut his teeth on Wall Street, and has been in the Far East since 1973.

From 1978 to 1990 he was head of the Hong Kong office of Drexel Burnham Lambert during its heyday as one of the world's largest investment banking firms. Since 1990 he has been president of Swiss Asian Investment Consultants.

So he's bullish on Asia, right? Not exactly. Lately Dr. Faber has been directing investors into selected Latin American markets. The profits there will make your eyes pop.

In 1987, convinced that Asian markets were headed for a crash, he recommended Chile. Since then, Chilean stocks have risen more than 385% in U.S. dollar terms.

On Dec. 12, 1988, the headline on his *Strategic Investment* column was "Argentina — A Treasure Among Depressed Markets." Dr. Faber reported that in Argentina, the economic pendulum had swung toward the side of extreme undervaluation. He pointed out that the market had gone up about 95% in the previous year, yet stocks were still selling for only three or four times earnings!

Argentine stocks, he said, were selling "at about an 80% discount. . ."

A year later, those stocks had tripled.

It may not seem possible to repeat a feat like that. But Marc Faber did so.

On Jan. 26, 1991, Dr. Faber once again spotted bargain basement values in a Latin American country. He asserted that Brazilian shares were going for half their worth, and advised *Strategic Investment* readers to get into the Brazil Fund (an easy-to-buy "country fund" that trades on the New York Stock Exchange.)

The Brazil Fund was at $8.25. It then went to $21.50—a 160% profit.

In upcoming issues, Dr. Faber will explain how to avoid the coming bloodbath in U.S. stocks and bonds. He'll tell you how to use your own local broker to buy global stocks that are growing twice as fast as most U.S. companies. . . stocks that are easy to trade through ADRs and plenty safe. . .stocks that could easily bring you 25% to 50% annual profits.

A Real-Life Indiana Jones
—Dr. Jack Wheeler—

One of *Strategic Investment*'s most colorful agents is Dr. Jack Wheeler, a man *The Washington Post* called a real-life Indiana Jones. He's practically a legend in the intelligence community. He personally discovered three tribes that had never before been contacted by civilization. And he is the only person

listed in the *Guinness Book of Records* to sky
dive at the North Pole.

Dr. Wheeler's love for adventure began
when he was a boy. He climbed the Matterhorn
when he was 14, swam the Hellespont at 16,
and lived with Mongol nomads in the Gobi
Desert at an age when getting a date on
Saturday night was the big adventure for
most people.

He's a veteran of six anti-communist
guerrilla conflicts. And he is credited by many
insiders for inspiring the "Reagan Doctrine"
that supported freedom fighters.

Somehow in the midst of all this he found
time to earn a doctorate of philosophy, to
write a book, to be the subject of a Dewar's
Scotch profile and to serve as an Arctic loca-
tion advisor to Clint Eastwood during the
filming of *Foxfire* in Greenland.

Profit from Being the First to Know

An unconventional source for an investment publication? Yes, but a very good one.
Dr. Wheeler, and other contacts like him,
make up our "distant early warning system"
. . .bringing you valuable news long before it
runs in your daily newspaper.

We never know where Dr. Wheeler will
turn up, as evidenced by this communique he
wired us three days before the Persian Gulf
War began:

"It will be short: the greatest amount
of violence in the shortest amount of
time in the history of warfare."

How did he know, when everyone else
was predicting a long, drawn-out bloodbath?
We don't pry, and he likes it that way.

His other calls have been equally remarkable. As early as 1985, Dr. Wheeler was
forecasting the demise of the Soviet Union.
His "reports from the front" may one day
rank as some of the most exciting "you are
there" journalism of the last ten years. He
reported in detail on military desertions,
economic turmoil and other signs of Soviet
collapse — months and even years before the
mainstream media.

In Feb. '89, a full ten months before the
Berlin Wall came down, Wheeler reported,
"The focus of struggle has now shifted to
Eastern Europe and inside the Soviet Union
itself. Our prediction is that it is entirely
possible that Moscow will lose its East European colonies. . ."

What's Next?

So what do Dr. Wheeler's worldwide intelligence sources tell him now? He sees India and Pakistan suffering the same "revolt
against the center" that finished the Soviet

Union. They'll be gone as we know them within a decade.

He sees Iran flexing its muscle in OPEC ...and the first sign may occur when we sight one of the nuclear subs Iran purchased from Russia off the coast of California.

"We are living in epochal history now," says Jack Wheeler. "Entirely new geopolitcal structures are being created before our eyes."

Get details in upcoming issues of *Strategic Investment*.

&

Forecast for the Millennium

We may not see the end of the world, but some earth-shaking events are going to take place as we approach the year 2000. Here's why.

Some time ago an amazing device was invented. It revolutionized the world.

This new device spread throughout the advanced countries with amazing speed. Within a generation, they were in every community. Thanks to the new invention, the cost of information fell to a fraction of what it used to be.

Ordinary people had more information sitting on their desktops than wealthy people once had in their expensive private libraries. What's more, people were able to spread their knowledge with amazing rapidity. Word of a new discovery or a revolution in one city would spread to distant cities almost instantly.

Where before governments and powerful organizations had controlled information, now almost everyone had it. Individuals obtained power they had never had before. One of Europe's most powerful empires came under challenge from its own people. Terrible wars raged. Whole new forms of government and organization had to arise to cope with the new information technology.

Am I talking about the computer, the microchip? Could be, but what I actually had in mind was the invention of movable type around 1450.

You probably learned in school that Johann Gutenberg invented modern printing somewhere back then. But you probably didn't learn the way it reshaped the whole world.

Once again, I'm trying to make a point. There are patterns in history. There's a way of understanding what's going on. But you won't find it on the evening news or in the pabulum spooned out by politicians.

We think we live in the age of rapid change and everything is new and different. But printing technology in its day spread just about as fast as the microchip and had much the same impact.

A few decades after the invention of movable type, a man named Martin Luther decided to defy the Roman church with his

"95 Theses." Within weeks, the printing press had spread his views all over Germany. Within months he was known throughout Europe.

Before the printing press, no one would have heard of Luther's ideas. Probably the authorities would have silenced him. He might have been executed.

But instead the new techology ushered in a new age. A new class of people acquired wealth and power. An older class lost out. Wars and revolutions swept Europe.

The 500-Year Cycle

The longest cycles in history last about 500 years. No one knows precisely why this is. I believe we'll eventually uncover a scientific explanation.

But I do know that the cycle is unusually precise. Around 500 A.D. the Roman Empire collapsed. About 1000 A.D. the Dark Ages gave way to the Middle Ages. And around 1500, the Modern Age began — ushered in by Gutenberg, Luther, da Vinci, and Columbus; by gunpowder and the printing press.

We're now at the turning point of that great 500-year cycle. We're also at the turning point of a 60-year cycle marked by crashes and depressions. There have been nine depressions, spaced about 60 years apart, since the mid-16th Century.

Mind you, people didn't know in 1550 that they were living in the Modern Age. They didn't know in 1930 that they were in a Great Depression — everyone thought it would blow over soon.

People generally don't understand what's happening while it's happening. The service we provide at STRATEGIC INVESTMENT is to explain the big picture and tie it into specific ways you can make money and protect yourself.

The Big Cycles Drive Change

To most people, what's going on in Russia is just a jumble of events that doesn't make any sense. Leaders hold summits, legislatures argue, people demonstrate in the streets. One minute the Russians were ten feet tall, the next minute they were beggars.

It all had something to do with Reagan and Gorbachev, but you don't quite know what. And meanwhile you have to earn your living and make the mortgage payments.

We're all distracted by a motion picture that runs 24 hours a day. It's called the "news."

Here at STRATEGIC INVESTMENT

things are a little bit different. We knew communism was going to collapse. And we said so before Gorbachev even came to power.

As quoted in *The Wall Street Journal*:

"In their 1987 book, *Blood in the Streets*, James Davidson and Sir William Rees-Mogg predicted a communist crack-up by noting that while the Soviet Union could turn in respectable rates of growth so long as it was industrializing, it was doomed once the world economy shifted from slabs of steel to producing complex silicon chips."

The Soviet Union was doomed by a new technology the same way feudal Europe was doomed by Gutenberg's press. It's the sort of new technology that usually appears at turning points of the great cycles.

"Megapolitics" is the name we've given to our unique way of looking at things.

The Great Wealth Transfer

Steam, assembly lines, interchangeable parts — they added up to a whole new system of making things. The factory system came about, and with it the Industrial Revolution,

which started about the same time as the
American and French Revolutions.

The Industrial Revolution created a new
class of millionaires in Britain and redefined
the meaning of wealth. But as late as 1870,
the country was still run by aristocrats whose
wealth was based on land.

750 families owned enormous estates of
10,000 to 30,000 acres. Make no mistake,
they were rich. The new industrialists had
immense wealth, too, but they still lacked
political power.

But those aristocrats made a big mistake when they failed to understand the
Megapolitics of their day.

They lost their status because new
technologies opened up North America and
turned it into the breadbasket of the world.
The McCormick reaper made it possible for
one man to do the work of ten (one of the
reasons the North won the American Civil
War). The steam railroad carried this massive
bounty of grain to America's ports, where
steamships carried it to Britain (a journey
that used to take weeks by sail).

Cheap grain caused British land values
to collapse. The landowners who had placed
their bets on the old technology fell. By 1910
the power of the aristocrats was broken.

You can call it coincidence if you like. . .
but the 1870s — when British land values

started to collapse — was a turning point in the 60-year cycle I mentioned earlier. There was a worldwide depression.

The Slow-Motion Depression

Yogi Berra's famous line, "It's deja vu all over again," is a good description of these 60-year cycles. Beware of the idea that the events of our time are unprecedented. Chances are there's plenty of precedent.

In fact, the parallels are uncanny.

Bank failures didn't start in the 1930s. They started in the 1920s, when the economy was booming and the stock market was going straight up. The same pattern began recurring in the '80s.

In the '20s as in the '80s, credit became easier and easier. At the beginning of the '20s, real estate lenders demanded 40% down. By the end of the '20s, huge loans were made, nothing down, on a hole in the ground. Second and third mortgages, backed by nothing, were sold to individual investors for twice the interest you could earn on a T-bill. People were told these were perfectly safe, that there had never been a default.

The same kind of thing went on in the stock market. People could borrow as much as they wished to invest in securities. The premise was that everything would always go up.

Then came the Great Depression. And
people found out everything doesn't always
go up.

We've had a crash in '87, a wave of bank
and S&L failures, a plunge in real estate
values. Yet it seems we're not in a depression.
This is confusing — can it be the doomsayers
are wrong?

I don't believe so. The difference this
time is that the federal government has a
massive role in our economy that it did not
yet have in the 1920s and early '30s. Reagan,
Bush and now Clinton have spent $4 trillion
and more to avoid the inevitable bust.

They will not succeed. All they have done
is to disguise the bust and stretch it out.
They've liquidated our nation's wealth and
impoverished generations to come in order to
keep the party going. But the party is about
to end. When the last dollar has been borrowed
and the last watch has been pawned for
another loan, when we can no longer pay
even the interest, the bust will come.

"Accidents" do happen. . .

History is full of examples of a whole of
way of life disappearing overnight.

In 380 A.D., everyday life in the city of
Rome was much the same as it had been for
hundreds of years. Only 30 years later that

way of life was over — gone forever. The city was sacked, the whole empire was overrun by primitive tribes. (They were that era's version of gang members who think fighting and stealing beats working.)

Cities were razed to the ground, their people sold into slavery. And they were the lucky ones — others were raped or killed on the spot.

In Russia in 1917, wealthy "liberals" cheered the fall of the czar. A few months later they found themselves being lined up and shot. Others froze or starved, forced to scrabble for a crust of bread as the whole society fell apart.

Everyday life is fragile. In a big city, if the trucks don't come in every morning with food, you don't eat. Period. If one or two key powerlines are cut, there's no light. It will take far less than you think to disrupt the comfortable life we take for granted.

As recently as 1944, German barons called "junkers" lorded over huge estates tilled by thousands of peasants — as they had for 700 years. A year later it was all gone. Everything. First reduced to rubble by the war, then given as spoils to the Poles and Russians.

Aristocrats and merchants were usually killed outright when the first wave of Russians came through. Manor houses were looted and

burned or taken over by the new landlords.
Millions of people were beaten, robbed and
raped — not just once, but over and over, as
they tried to make their way to the West.
Hundreds of thousands died.

It can happen here

Lurid tales that have nothing to with us?
Maybe.

But I happen to think the next few years
may not be so easy on "the rich" here in
America. If my estimate of the situation is
correct — and I believe it is — the next few
years won't be easy on *anyone*. But "the rich"
will be singled out for special treatment, as
they were in past depressions.

After all, we have a President who
enourages resentment against "the rich." As
though people need encouragement.

I foresee the deepest economic downturn
since the '30s. And I believe, when it comes,
that the social fabric of America will be tested
to the limit.

The riots last year in Los Angeles are
just a small taste of what is to come. Lord
Rees-Mogg and I predicted them.

What will the next wave of riots be like?
According to the *Washington Post,* 1.9 million AK-47 automatic rifles were imported
from China between 1989 and 1991 alone.

Rees-Mogg and I have also warned again and again that America is vulnerable to terrorism. The attack on New York's World Trade Center validates our warning. And once more, it's just a taste of what's to come.

It's worth taking a closer look at this incident. This was no carefully planned, high-tech caper. It was a homemade bomb from materials you and I could buy off the shelf. The driver was such an amateur he went back to the truck rental agency to claim the deposit on the van he blew up.

Act Now and Profit
Even if I'm Wrong

Things may not get as bad as the fall of Rome — let me be the first to admit. But they don't have to get nearly that bad to upset your life and all the plans you've made.

As far as your investments go, there's little upside, and enormous downside. Even the wildest optimists don't think the Dow is going up another 10% this year. Meanwhile, a plunge of 25% is easily possible. At 25% off, stocks *still* would not be cheap. Their value would be just about right.

The steps I want you to take are extremely simple. Get out of debt. Get out of "rosy scenario" stocks and bonds that depend on tomorrow being just like today. Shake off the complacency that says it can't happen here and the Dow is going to 4000.

Fires seldom happen, but I bet you still own fire insurance. Reading STRATEGIC INVESTMENT is a form of insurance.

Subscribe to STRATEGIC INVEST-MENT for a year. Keep abreast of the ominous trends I've described. The worst that can happen is you'll have an exclusive insider's pipeline into the Oval Office, 10 Downing Street, the Kremlin and countless board-rooms, presidential palaces and intelligence agencies.

The best that can happen is you'll profit from the bullet-proof investments I've iden-tified that will be extremely profitable no matter what happens — inflation, depression or healthy growth.

See page 115 for information on how to order.

꙳

No-Risk Introductory Subscription Offer

(For new subscribers only)

☐ **YES!** Rush all five FREE reports and enter my one-year (12 issues) introductory subscription to *Strategic Investment* for $59 (regularly $109). (See reverse for more about FREE reports.) Plus, I may cancel anytime before my fourth issue and receive all my money back, or anytime thereafter for a prorated refund on remaining issues. In either case, the reports are mine to keep.

☐ **BEST DEAL:** I prefer a two-year subscription to *Strategic Investment* for $118 because that way I can receive the hardcover bestseller *The Great Reckoning* in addition to the five bonus reports.

☐ My payment for $59 ($118 for two years) is enclosed.
(Make checks payable to Agora, Inc. MD residents add 5% sales tax.)

Daytime Phone Number: _____
(for order confirmation only)

Name _____

Address _____

City/State/Zip _____

☐ Charge my credit card: ☐ VISA
        ☐ MasterCard ☐ AMEX

Card Number: _____

Expiration Date: _____

Signature: _____

SIBK993

Strategic Investment • 824 East Baltimore Street • Baltimore, MD 21202 or fax (410)539-7348

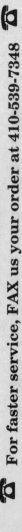

No-Risk Introductory Subscription Offer

(For new subscribers only)

☐ **YES!** Rush all five FREE reports and enter my one-year (12 issues) introductory subscription to *Strategic Investment* for $59 (regularly $109). (See reverse for more about FREE reports.) Plus, I may cancel anytime before my fourth issue and receive all my money back, or anytime thereafter for a prorated refund on remaining issues. In either case, the reports are mine to keep.

☐ **BEST DEAL:** I prefer a two-year subscription to *Strategic Investment* for $118 because that way I can receive the hardcover bestseller *The Great Reckoning* in addition to the five bonus reports.

☐ My payment for $59 ($118 for two years) is enclosed.
(Make checks payable to Agora, Inc. MD residents add 5% sales tax.)

☐ Charge my credit card: ☐ VISA
    ☐ MasterCard   ☐ AMEX

Card Number: _____

Expiration Date: _____

Signature: _____

Daytime Phone Number: _____
(for order confirmation only)

Name _____

Address _____

City/State/Zip _____

Strategic Investment • 824 East Baltimore Street • Baltimore, MD 21202 or fax (410)539-7348

SIBK993

Sign up for a one-year, no-risk trial subscription to *Strategic Investment*, at a $50 savings, and you'll receive your 5 FREE bonus reports:

How to Profit During the Coming Debt Default • The Clinton Years •
The $138,000 Estate Tax Surprise • The Strategic Investment Income Portfolio •
Investing in The Real Estate Crisis

FREE with your two-year subscription

The hardcover bestseller *The Great Reckoning*. The chief editors of Strategic Investment summarize a lifetime of studying the forces of history. Then they distill it into specific forecasts and investment advice. An invaluable companion to your monthly issues of their newsletter.

100% Money-Back Guarantee

If you're not completely satisfied with *Strategic Investment*, just let us know anytime before you receive your fourth issue and we'll refund the entire amount of your subscription. Promptly. With no questions asked. You don't have to send back the special reports. . .they're yours to keep, along with all issues you've received.

If you cancel after receiving four or more issues, we'll send you a prorated refund for all unmailed issues. . .and, again, you keep the bonus reports.

 For faster service, FAX us your order at 410-539-7348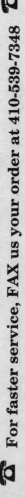

No-Risk Introductory Subscription Offer

(For new subscribers only)

☐ **YES!** Rush all five FREE reports and enter my one-year (12 issues) introductory subscription to *Strategic Investment* for $59 (regularly $109). (See reverse for more about FREE reports.) Plus, I may cancel anytime before my fourth issue and receive all my money back, or anytime thereafter for a prorated refund on remaining issues. In either case, the reports are mine to keep.

☐ **BEST DEAL:** I prefer a two-year subscription to *Strategic Investment* for $118 because that way I can receive the hardcover bestseller *The Great Reckoning* in addition to the five bonus reports.

☐ My payment for $59 ($118 for two years) is enclosed.
(Make checks payable to Agora, Inc. MD residents add 5% sales tax.)

☐ Charge my credit card: ☐ VISA ☐ MasterCard ☐ AMEX

Daytime Phone Number: _____
(for order confirmation only)

Card Number: _____

Expiration Date: _____

Signature: _____

Name _____

Address _____

City/State/Zip _____

Strategic Investment • 824 East Baltimore Street • Baltimore, MD 21202 or fax (410)539-7348

SIBK993

Sign up for a one-year, no-risk trial subscription to *Strategic Investment*, at a $50 savings, and you'll receive your 5 FREE bonus reports:

How to Profit During the Coming Debt Default • The Clinton Years •
The $138,000 Estate Tax Surprise • The Strategic Investment Income Portfolio •
Investing in The Real Estate Crisis

100% Money-Back Guarantee

If you're not completely satisfied with *Strategic Investment*, just let us know anytime before you receive your fourth issue and we'll refund the entire amount of your subscription. Promptly. With no questions asked. You don't have to send back the special reports. . .they're yours to keep, along with all issues you've received.

If you cancel after receiving four or more issues, we'll send you a prorated refund for all unmailed issues. . .and, again, you keep the bonus reports.

FREE with your two-year subscription

The hardcover bestseller *The Great Reckoning*. The chief editors of Strategic Investment summarize a lifetime of studying the forces of history. Then they distill it into specific forecasts and investment advice. An invaluable companion to your monthly issues of their newsletter.

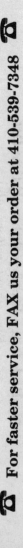 For faster service, FAX us your order at 410-539-7348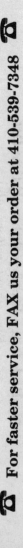

No-Risk Introductory Subscription Offer
(For new subscribers only)

☐ **YES!** Rush all five FREE reports and enter my one-year (12 issues) introductory subscription to *Strategic Investment* for $59 (regularly $109). (See reverse for more about FREE reports.) Plus, I may cancel anytime before my fourth issue and receive all my money back, or anytime thereafter for a prorated refund on remaining issues. In either case, the reports are mine to keep.

☐ **BEST DEAL:** I prefer a two-year subscription to *Strategic Investment* for $118 because that way I can receive the hardcover bestseller *The Great Reckoning* in addition to the five bonus reports.

☐ My payment for $59 ($118 for two years) is enclosed.
(Make checks payable to Agora, Inc. MD residents add 5% sales tax.)

Daytime Phone Number: _____
(for order confirmation only)

Name _____

Address _____

City/State/Zip _____

☐ Charge my credit card: ☐ VISA
    ☐ MasterCard ☐ AMEX

Card Number: _____

Expiration Date: _____

Signature: _____

SIBK993

Strategic Investment • 824 East Baltimore Street • Baltimore, MD 21202 or fax (410)539-7348

Sign up for a one-year, no-risk trial subscription to *Strategic Investment*, at a $50 savings, and you'll receive your 5 FREE bonus reports:

How to Profit During the Coming Debt Default • The Clinton Years • The $138,000 Estate Tax Surprise • The Strategic Investment Income Portfolio • Investing in The Real Estate Crisis

FREE with your two-year subscription

The hardcover bestseller *The Great Reckoning*. The chief editors of Strategic Investment summarize a lifetime of studying the forces of history. Then they distill it into specific forecasts and investment advice. An invaluable companion to your monthly issues of their newsletter.

☎ For faster service, FAX us your order at 410-539-7348 ☎